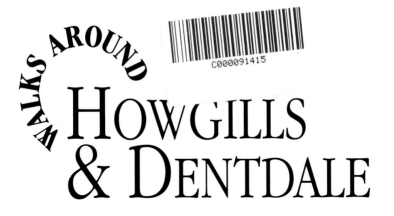

WALKS AROUND

HOWGILLS & DENTDALE

TEN GREAT WALKS UNDER SIX MILES

Sheila Bowker

Dalesman

First published in 2012 by Dalesman
an imprint of
Country Publications Ltd
The Water Mill
Broughton Hall
Skipton
North Yorkshire BD23 3AG
www.dalesman.co.uk

Cover: Cautley Crag & Cautley Spout by Wayne Hutchinson

ISBN 978-1-85568-305-1

Printed in China by Latitude Press Ltd.

PUBLISHER'S NOTE

The information given in this book has been provided in good faith and is intended
only as a general guide. Whilst all reasonable efforts have been made to ensure that
details were correct at the time of publication, the author and Country Publications
Ltd cannot accept any responsibility for inaccuracies. It is the responsibility of
individuals undertaking outdoor activities to approach the activity with caution and,
especially if inexperienced, to do so under appropriate supervision. The activity
described in this book is strenuous and individuals should ensure that they are
suitably fit before embarking upon it. They should carry the appropriate equipment
and maps, be properly clothed and have adequate footwear. They should also take
note of weather conditions and forecasts, and leave notice of their intended route
and estimated time of return.

Contents

Introduction

Although admired by many travelling the M6 or West Coast mainline railway through the Lune Gorge, the Howgill Fells remain as rather secretive and secluded hidden treasure; but to be among them is to be surrounded by them, as they hug close like huge, camouflage-coloured velvet cushions. For the Howgills huddle together in a smooth, rounded, upland mass, and the reason for their smooth outlines is the hardness of the rock coupled with minimal glacial erosion. The Fells are surrounded on all sides by the winding rivers of the Lune, Eden, Rawthey and Clough, and walks in this book take you along sections of these beautiful rivers.

The Howgill Fells take their name from a small settlement in the Lune Valley where a number of homesteads, a woollen mill employing up to a hundred, and a church once thrived. Sadly, the Howgill of today consists of just one farm. The fells are home to hardy Rough Fell sheep, and small free-roaming ponies in piebald shades of brown and cream.

Dentdale may only be 10½ miles (17 km) long, but it packs some superb scenery into that short distance, and in a way that looks and feels different, for it acts as border country, creating a dividing line between the Lake District and the Yorkshire Dales either side, yet with a landscape and architecture dissimilar to both. Being a touch more gentle, a touch more green, Dentdale has a natural, unpretentious individuality about it.

The lovely River Dee runs through the valley, as does the Dent Fault. The fault is a fracture of the Earth's crust caused when landmasses collided about 250 million years ago, and which marks the geological boundary between the 340-million-year-old Carboniferous limestone of the Craven Dales to the south, and the 425-million-year-old Silurian rock to the north, of which the Howgill Fells are made.

Some walks in this book have steep sections, and may be muddy underfoot after rain, so boots are advisable. Rainwear, plus emergency food and drink, should always be carried. Take a good map and compass, and know how to use them. Recommended maps are the OS Explorer OL2 and OL19, as specified for each walk. Take all litter home with you, close gates (unless clearly propped open), keep dogs on leads at all times, and keep to public paths. For details of public transport, visit www.dalesbus.org.

Barbon and the River Lune

> **Distance: 4½ miles (7 km). Time: 2½ hours.**
> **Start/parking: car park beside Hodge Bridge, just off the A683**
> **Kirkby Lonsdale–Sedbergh road; grid ref 624826.**
> **Terrain: footpaths, bridleways and quiet lanes. Height gained: 200 feet (60 m).**
> **Public transport: none available.**
> **Facilities: pub; picnic seating outside Barbon village hall.**
> **Map: OS Explorer OL2 – Yorkshire Dales Southern and Western.**

Although the OS map indicates that Hodge Bridge is not Roman, sections of the A683 are in fact constructed along the route of the Roman road that provided access to the Roman fort on the northern bank of Leck Beck at Over Barrow, one mile (1.5 km) to the west of Cowan Bridge.

Leave the car park. Turn right on the main road to cross Hodge Bridge as it spans Barbon Beck. Turn immediately left on a footpath confirmed with a sign. The path bears slightly left towards the beck, and continues along the right-hand bank with Kirkby Lonsdale golf course on the right. (Beware of the beck's overhanging edges – and badly struck golf balls.)

At the end of a wall on the left, follow a signed bridleway between the beck and the wall. At a meeting of footpaths, ignore the footpath sign straight ahead and turn left across a narrow fairway. Turn right on a grassy track just before a footbridge. The next fairway is soon reached. The path crosses to the right in front of a raised tee and continues close to trees on the right.

Where the trees veer away to the right, carry straight on towards the beck (enjoying good views of Barbon Low Fell on the left). Keep down on the narrow path through bushes to the left of the golf course. After a short distance, cross a fence-stile into a field with a large patch of rushes in the centre. The path is indistinct here, but bear right, round the reeds, aiming for a meeting of walls along the field. The path becomes clearer as the beck comes close on the left and the land on the right rises up fairly steeply.

Keep to the left of Beckfoot Farm. Cross Barbon Beck via either a concrete bridge straight ahead or the more attractive arched packhorse bridge to the left. Follow Lowfields Lane south to the tiny hamlet of Low Beckfoot. Turn right just prior to a copse of trees along a track signposted 'River Lune'.

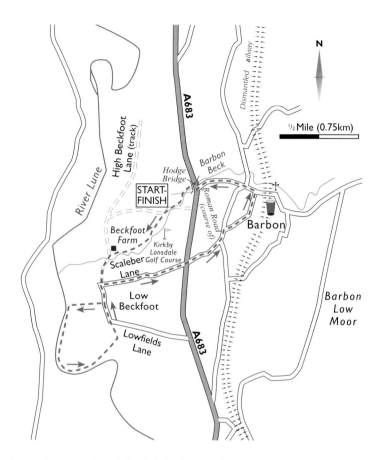

Leave the track where it bends left after crossing a cattle grid, to go straight ahead on an indistinct path across a large field towards a line of trees and telegraph cables. Go through a gate in the far right-hand corner leading to the bank of the Lune. Turn left.

Take time to enjoy this delightful section of the river. The word 'Lune' is derived from a Celtic word meaning 'health giving'. The river's source is up on the edge of the Pennines on Ravenstonedale Common, and the most famous section of the river is the Lune Gorge just south of Tebay, where the river negotiates a narrow valley which carries both the M6 motorway and the main West Coast railway line.

6

The grey wagtail can be spotted on fast-flowing stretches of rivers and streams.

The path crosses back into a field but carries on alongside the river. At the bridge, walk up round the buttresses but don't cross.

This superb castellated and gargoyled bridge was built to take the residents of Underley Hall to the railway station at Barbon.

Continue along the edge of a large field with the river still on your right, confirmed by yellow marker-posts. Towards the end of the field, bear left to cut the corner. A faint track in the grass soon becomes more apparent.

Skirting round the property ahead, pass through the second small gate on the right. Join the lane by a footpath sign. (The route here shown on OS maps has been diverted.) Turn left under the bridge along Lowfields Lane and back through Low Beckfoot. Take the first lane on the right (Scaleber Lane), from where there are good views of the Howgill Fells to the left.

Continue past the golf clubhouse on the left. Go straight over at the cross-roads along a lane, crossing the route of the old Roman road. Bear left where the lane splits, signposted 'Barbon and Dent'. Bear right at the next junction into Barbon.

Barbon village is mentioned in Domesday Book as Berebrune, and its church, St Bartholomew's, was built in the Perpendicular style in 1893. It's reputed to have views of the fells from its east window good enough to render the lengthiest sermon bearable.

Turn left in the village and follow this lane back to Hodge Bridge.

Dent and Barbondale

Distance: 4½ miles (7 km). **Time:** 2½ hours.
Start/parking: national park car park in Dent; grid ref 704871.
Terrain: footpaths, bridleways and quiet lanes. **Height gained:** 1,100 feet (335 m).
Public transport: bus 564B connects Kendal, Sedbergh and Oxenholme
Station with Dent.
Facilities: Dent has the usual village amenities.
Map: OS Explorer OL2 – Yorkshire Dales Southern and Western.

From the Dales National Park car park in Dent, cross the lane and walk straight ahead up to the green. Keep ahead in the same direction, signposted 'Flinter Gill'. (Observe an elaborate kissing-gate on the right, as this is your return route.) Walk up Flinter Gill's stony track.

Flinter Gill is an outreach of Dent Village Heritage Centre, with signs notifying the areas of historical interest (picking up a leaflet from the centre before leaving the village could be useful). There are dancing flags (where fabric was wet during the weaving process), a wishing tree, limekiln and waterfalls. It's worth visiting High Laning Farm barn (signposted just off on the right) to see the displays and photographs of old farming implements.

As the trees are cleared, the track levels considerably and makes a delightful walk over open moorland.

A stile in the fence on the right leads up to an elevated viewpoint at High Ground, where a toposcope helps identify the extensive panorama.

A well-placed seat is at the T-junction with Occupation Road (marked on the map as Green Lane/Track). Turn right, signposted 'Keldishaw 1½ miles'.

Originally an old droving road, Occupation Road was rebuilt as an access route for farmers to reach their allotted land following the Enclosures of 1859 when common grazing land was divided and walls built. Occupation Road is a wide, walled, stony track and is great high-level walking.

After crossing High Lathe Gill you reach South Lord's Land; good views left along Barbondale can be enjoyed. Turn right at the T-junction with Barbondale Road at Keldishaw. As the lane gently twists down through shrubby trees, enjoy the views across Dentdale.

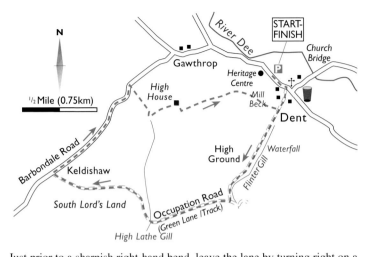

Just prior to a sharpish right-hand bend, leave the lane by turning right on a path signposted 'Dent 1¼ miles' and 'Gawthrop ¾ mile via High House'. The wide, stony track swings right, round a barn. Cross a beck. A wall comes in on the left and reedy fields to the right. A deep, wooded valley shelters a gill to the left. The track swings sharp left over the gill, then rises up across open fields, with good views to the Howgill Fells on the left.

The route keeps left (confirmed by yellow markers) round High House and its rather mucky farmyard. Descend gently, whilst bearing right towards a beck for a short distance. Cross a clapper bridge. Rise, equally gently, up the opposite bank. At a stile where the path divides, take the right-hand option, signposted 'Dent'. Cross a field by aiming just to the left of a barn ahead. Work round to the left of the barn via a couple of stiles. Follow the direction of a yellow arrow to cross the next field diagonally. The path descends gently down numerous fields connected by stiles, all with yellow arrows; the roofs of Dent village can soon be seen down on the right.

Cross a stile over a fence, followed by wooden steps. Go down to a track just before the first building (a barn) is reached. Turn right along the track. A gate leads into Mill Beck farmyard. Just beyond the farm, keep ahead to meet a yellow-arrowed telegraph pole. This indicates the route to the right. Cross a beck via a plank bridge. Keep uphill across the next field. Exit on to a track at the point where it bends sharply. Turn left along the track for a few strides. Leave it to keep ahead on a footpath with a fence on the left. Continue for a short distance to join the lane via the kissing-gate passed on the outward route. Turn left back into Dent.

9

Cowgill circular

Distance: 5 miles (8 km). Time: 2½–3 hours.
Start/parking: parking area approximately 1 mile (1.5 km) west of Cowgill
on the unclassified lane on the north side of Dentdale between Cowgill
and Dent; grid ref 743866.
Terrain: footpaths, bridleways and quiet lanes. Height gained: 760 feet (230 m).
Public transport: trains on the Settle-Carlisle line stop at Dent Station,
approximately ¾ mile (1.25 km) east of Cowgill; bus 564B connects
Kendal, Sedbergh and Oxenholme Station with Cowgill.
Facilities: none available.
Map: OS Explorer OL2 – Yorkshire Dales Southern and Western.

From the parking area, turn left. Walk along the lane with the River Dee on
your left. (Observe the footpath on the right that comes down the drive from
Broadfield House, as this is the return route.)

*The River Dee, formed at Dent Head from becks and gills running off Blea
Moor, flows northwards to Cowgill before bearing left through Dentdale.*

The lane rises gently past the phone and post boxes in front of Gibbs Hall.

*Gibbs Hall, a very handsome building now sadly in ruin, dates back to the
sixteenth century, and is described in David Boulton's booklet* Discovering
Upper Dentdale *as once being the hub of a flourishing tannery business.*

Turn left off the lane opposite Basil Busk Farm on the footpath signposted
'Lenny's Leap ¼ mile'. The path dog-legs left and descends down a field.
Turn right on the Dales Way. Proceed across pastureland with the river close
on the left. Cross Tommy Bridge. Turn left, signposted 'Sike Fold'. Walk
along the riverbank for a short distance. After a gate, turn right up a high-
walled track. Exit on the lane running along the southern side of the dale.

Turn left along the lane. Joining the Dales Way route again, turn right up the
farm track to Laithbank. A sign on a post to the right-hand side of the track
confirms the route. The track swings left. A signpost to Clint leads you on a
narrow footpath round a barn and over a beck via a plank bridge.

*There are views ahead of Dent Station and the Settle-Carlisle line. At 1,150 feet
(350 m) above sea-level, the station is the highest on any mainline railway.*

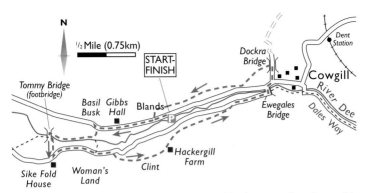

The path continues along the dale now at roughly the same elevation and in the same direction; regular yellow markers confirm the way. Skirt round the rear of a property and over open fields. Cross the corner of a small field furnished with new kissing-gates. Turn left along a lane for a short distance. As the lane bears left, leave it via the footpath on the right. The path now descends gently through an area of new plantation, and soon ends as it rejoins the lane. Turn right and walk to Ewegales Bridge. Leave the Dales Way route as it continues ahead, by turning left over the bridge and past Cowgill Church.

Cowgill Church was built in 1837-8 and the foundation stone was laid by Dent-born Adam Sedgwick, Professor of Geology at Cambridge University.

Cross a second bridge. Turn left along a gated lane with a 'No Through Road' sign. Soon after the lane becomes a track and crosses a beck, leave it and take a path on the left bearing very slightly left across a field. The path then continues in the same direction with a wall on the left. It crosses a farm track and a tiny ford. Still heading towards the lane running along the north side of the dale, the path crosses a stile just before reaching a large farm, then heads away uphill again. It then continues in roughly the same direction along the northern slopes of the dale.

Keep between the buildings at Spice Gill Farm. Bear right towards the end of the farmyard, then left up steps and over a beck. The path maintains altitude past a white-washed property. Yellow markers then lead you uphill on a track with a barn up on the right. As the track swings right, leave it to follow yellow markers pointing left into the farmyard at Allen Haw. After crossing a couple more fields, descend a stony gully and cross a bridge over a beck. Rise up past Hollins. Continue in the same direction with a wall on the right to work round Broadfield House. Follow the track downhill to the lane. Turn left back to the parking area.

An exploration of Dentdale

Distance: 4¾ miles (7.5 km). **Time:** 3½ hours.
Start/parking: national park car park in Dent; grid ref 704871.
Terrain: footpaths, bridleways and quiet lanes. **Height gained:** 445 feet (135 m).
Public transport: bus 564B connects Kendal, Sedbergh and Oxenholme
Station with Dent.
Facilities: Dent has the usual village amenities.
Map: OS Explorer OL2 – Yorkshire Dales Southern and Western.

Turn right out of the car park along the lane until the River Dee comes close
on the right. Join the Dales Way footpath signposted to Barth Bridge. Walk
along the riverbank. Climb the steps up to the lane. Turn right across the
gracefully arched Barth Bridge. Follow the lane as it bears left alongside the
river. Leave the lane where it bends right, away from the river, by taking a
footpath to the left of a wide gate, signposted 'Mire House 1¼ miles'. The
path descends down steps and follows the raised floodbank beside the river.

*The valley has a very flat floor here, caused by a lake being formed through
glaciation during the last Ice Age.*

Continue along the floodbank. A footbridge and white farmhouse are passed
on the left then, after approximately another five minutes, cross a stile with
a waymarker pointing to the right and over a second stile. The footpath
heads across fields (which may be boggy) in the direction of the farm. Join
an obvious track which exits on to the lane by Mire House.

Turn right along the lane past Old Craft Barn at Helmside. Continue for one
more field and take the track on the left, signposted 'Rawridding'. Turn right
behind the first farmhouse on a waymarked concrete track uphill. Branch
left to a footpath sign by three gates. Continue ahead in the direction given
by the sign. Pass an isolated hawthorn. Arrive at more gates and another
footpath sign.

*The views across Dentdale are excellent from here onwards, with Whernside
ahead, and Great Coum and Combe Scar to the right.*

Follow the wall on your left to a large step-stile over a good example of a
laid hedge. Continue across two more fields with the wall up on the left. A
wide gate tucked in a corner by a telegraph pole leads to a walled track to

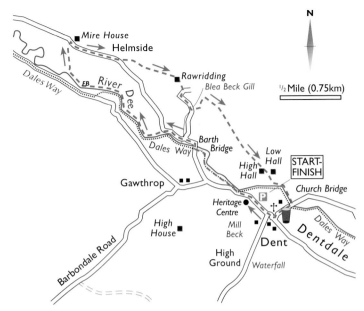

Rawridding Farm just ahead. Turn right before the farm on to a walled gravel track. At a junction, turn down a metalled lane to pass Hole House. Continue on the lane. Take a concrete track turning left and ascending, signposted 'Frostrow'.

By a solitary fir tree, turn left between the farm buildings at Hacra. Fork left into a walled lane. This leads to a footpath sign on the right. Go through a small gate leading into a field. Continue with a wall on the left to a stone stile. Head straight across the field to a small wooden gate in the wall. Here, keep on the higher ground, right of a patch of rushes, to a gated stile. Bear slightly right of the brow of the gentle hill ahead. A marker post directs the route down through large trees and rushes, and across boggy ground, to a second marker post and small wooden gate.

Bear left along a muddy track to pass between farm buildings. Cross a stile at the end of a wall on the left leading into a field with a large pond on the left. Keep ahead over two more fields; there are attractive views to Dent village. Aiming for the round chimneys of High Hall ahead, drop down and take the farm track between the buildings.

High Hall bears a plaque explaining it was rebuilt in 1625 and, although a sad sight now, it's reputed to have once been the grand manor house of Dent.

13

In Dent village is this memorial to Adam Sedgwick,
born in the village and who later became known as
the 'father of modern geology'.

Follow the track downhill, past waterfalls and Low Hall. Reach a lane, where you turn left for a short distance. Now cross a stile on the right leading to a path along the left bank of the River Dee. Take the steps up to the road at Church Bridge. Turn right along the lane, then right again through the village to the car park.

You'll pass the memorial to Dent's most famous son, Adam Sedgwick, who was the first person to discover and interpret the Dent Fault (see introduction on page 4). He was born at Dent Parsonage and, after attending university at Cambridge, went on to become Professor of Geology there in 1818. Sedgwick's pioneering research into the previously unexplored geology of this region and the older rock systems of Britain laid the foundation for modern geology.

Around Sedbergh

Distance: 3 miles (5 km). Time: 2 hours.
Start: beginning of the track to the left of Westwood Books, close to where Main Street joins the A684 towards the east of Sedbergh; grid ref 660922.
Parking: various car parking options in Sedbergh, ideally towards the more easterly part as that's where the start and finish of the walk are located.
Terrain: footpaths, bridleways, short road and lane sections.
Height gained: 570 feet (175 m).
Public transport: buses link Sedbergh with Brough, Kendal and Dent.
Facilities: Sedbergh has most small town amenities.
Map: OS Explorer OL19 – Howgill Fells & Upper Eden Valley.

Sedbergh, the centre of an area of dispersed Norse settlements, is a picturesque town of narrow streets and historic buildings lying at the foot of the Howgills. This walk provides a good introduction to the town.

Begin the walk by taking the track along the left of Westwood Books signposted 'Castlehaw'. This soon passes the site of a motte-and-bailey castle on the right (a permissive path allows access).

The Normans built a motte-and-bailey castle at Castlehaw to defend themselves against marauding Scots. In times of danger they gathered their animals into the bailey and themselves into the motte above.

Sedbergh is a good starting point for an exploration of the Howgill Fells.

15

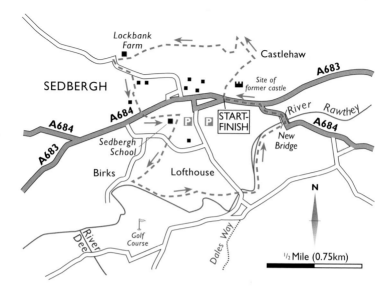

Stay on the track as it curves and ascends, and turns left immediately before a barn. Go over the bridge by Castlehaw House. Turn left again, signposted 'Jubilee Wood'.

Farming stock is being excluded from the ancient, sheltered woodland at Jubilee Wood to encourage natural regeneration and protect the area's diverse flora and fauna. The wood provides a valuable and increasingly threatened habitat for the flowers, ferns, birds and mammals which all find sanctuary here.

Follow the path through the woods with Settlebeck Gill on your left. Turn left and ford the beck where a signpost points 'To the Fell'. Follow a footpath to another sign to 'Joss Lane'. Turn left again, over a stile. A gate-stile then leads to a track on a bend. Join the track and turn right across a field. Where the track bends very sharply right, leave it to take the walled footpath straight ahead.

The path crosses fields just below Canada Wood, and continues in the same direction, crossing stiles on a waymarked path, to Lockbank farm. Proceed through the farmyard to reach Howgill Lane at a sharp bend. Turn left downhill for a short distance. Take a footpath across the road, between properties, signpoasted 'Cattle Market'. For a short while the walk becomes more suburban now, as the narrow path goes straight ahead to the A684

16

You may be lucky enough to spot a stoat in Jubilee Wood, near Sedbergh.

road. Turn left for a few paces, then take the path on the right through the gates of Sedbergh School, signposted 'Loftus Hill ¼ mile'.

Sedbergh School is a co-educational boarding school that's proud of its many ex-pupils who have gone on to make their mark in the fields of sport, arts and science. It was founded as a small chantry school in 1525 by Roger Lupton of Howgill, who was Canon of Windsor and Provost of Eton.

Keep left of the main school buildings to meet a junction of tracks. Take the sharp right-hand option, signposted 'Birks', which passes to the right of the sports field. Continue ahead through a kissing-gate on the left. Cross a green and go through another kissing-gate leading to Busk Lane. Cross straight over on the continuation of the track, again signposted to 'Birks', and with the rugby field on your right. Leave the track through a kissing-gate on the right opposite a barn, once again signposted 'Birks'. Follow the footpath straight ahead, which descends quite steeply to the River Rawthey. Turn left.

Follow the riverbank for a short distance, then leave it to head uphill, through a kissing-gate. Pass a ruin on a small hill to the right. The path keeps briefly to the left of woodland. A stile on the right leads you into the woods and meanders down along a well-signposted path. A stile then leads out to fields. The path bears left along a narrow field between properties to a lane, which you join to cross to the other side of the river. Now take the footpath on the left along the right-hand bank. Continue alongside this very attractive section of the Rawthey as far as New Bridge, where the main A684 road crosses. Turn left along the road back into Sedbergh.

Garsdale and Grisedale

Distance: 5¾ miles (9 km). Time: 3 hours.
Start/parking: adjacent to Garsdale Station; grid ref 788917.
Terrain: footpaths, tracks (some not distinct), and short road and lane
sections; this walk is challenging as Grisedale is a remote area, so would
be best enjoyed during a spell of dry weather and when there is clear
visibility; as open moorland is crossed, map-reading skills are essential.
Height gained: 830 feet (255 m).
Public transport: trains on the Settle-Carlisle line stop at Garsdale Station;
buses from Hawes stop at Garsdale Station.
Facilities: Moorcock Inn, approximately ¾ mile (1.25 km) from the start.
Map: OS Explorer OL19 – Howgill Fells & Upper Eden Valley.

*Sheltered to the north by the dark moors of Aisgill and Wild Boar Fell, and
to the west by Baugh Fell, Grisedale is an isolated upland valley that has a
wild and lonely feel to it.*

*Constructed during the 1870s, the Settle–Carlisle railway line irrevocably
altered the landscape and lives of the people along its route, none more so
than at Garsdale. In his book* Garsdale, *WR Mitchell describes it as a very
special station: "The only junction on the line, it had a turntable on which
locomotives spun out of control, a tank house also used as a social centre
and the highest water troughs in the world … t' junction was more than a
railway station, it was the pulse of a small community in which station-
master, signalmen and porters were heroes."*

From Garsdale Station, walk downhill. Cross the A684 road on to a footpath
signposted 'Grisedale 1 mile, Flust 2 miles'. Follow a tractor-track for a
short distance. Bear left on the narrow footpath heading along just above a
wall. The path ascends and crosses a stile. A direction arrow indicates the
route is straight ahead over moorland (keeping the railway station directly
behind you). There are good views of the curving beck down on the left as
the next stile is reached and where a sign assists the way forward.

The path bears left towards Blake Mire Farm and leads through a stile at the
right-hand end of the buildings. The route is less distinct as you cross a small
beck and then a stile in poor condition in a tumbled-down wall. Pass a barn
on your right. Maintain altitude over a field to come to a footpath sign. Head
downhill towards a ruined building by joining a track that swings down and

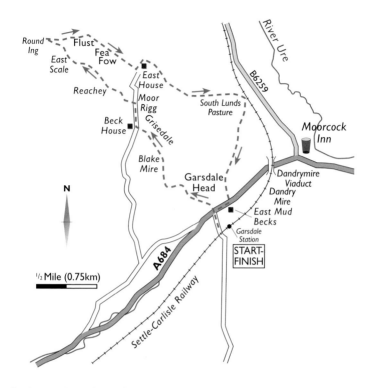

leads out through a wide gate on to Grisedale Road by a couple of properties.

Barry Cockcroft referred to Grisedale as 'The Dale that Died' in his book and the Yorkshire Television documentary he made about the dale. But the dale didn't die completely: a few of the farmhouses and dwellings are still inhabited, there are sheep in the fields, ducks on the beck and flowers in some of the gardens. Grisedale may not be as boisterous as it once was, but it's still alive.

Turn right and follow the lane uphill as far as the next property, Moor Rigg. Bear left on the footpath signposted 'East House via Round Ing'. Descend into a field. Keep on heading down towards Grisedale Beck, your companion on the left for a while now. The path proceeds with a broken-down wall on the right as you head upstream. The route leads away from the beck for a while to cross the track leading to Reachey. Go along a short flagged section, after which the path becomes grass again.

Waymarks confirm the route as the beck comes close again, but the beck loops away to the left as the path heads on towards the ruined buildings of East Scale, set in a small copse of trees.

This is a particularly attractive spot, with a pretty bridge and ruined buildings, and would make a nice picnic stop.

The beck is still close as you near a gate leading to a building. A footpath sign directs you uphill and away from the beck for the last time. The path is indistinct as you head towards another ruined building, which is set into a curve of a wall. There's another curve in the wall just beyond the ruin. You're now at the point where you head back, sharp right, and where signage points the way to East House.

Yellow waymarkers highlight the route as it heads towards the right-hand edge of a copse in the distance. Continue on to Flust. Go over a step-stile and turn immediately right, keeping the building on your left. Descend to a gate with a way-marker. Ford a small beck. Keep along with a fence on the right. As the fence ends, keep ahead towards the oddly named farm at Fea Fow. Keep to the right of the buildings. Join the farm track to its T-junction with a metalled lane just above East House.

Turn left and follow the lane as it swings uphill. Where the lane swings sharply left and becomes a gravel track, leave it by turning right on a tractor-track with a wall on the right which drops a short distance away after a while. You're heading over open moorland as you cross a ladder-stile. A wall is just away to the left as you descend the reedy land of South Lunds Pasture towards the railway footbridge. Don't cross the bridge. Instead, go through a gate on the right into a field. Follow the faint path that gradually bears away from the railway line. A ladder-stile leads out on to open moor. The path keeps on ahead across Garsdale Low Moor.

There are views here of Dandrymire Viaduct, which carries the Settle-Carlisle line across Garsdale Head. The viaduct is 227 yards (207 m) long and has 12 arches, and 50 feet (15 m) of digging down through soft peat was necessary to find bedrock for the pillars.

Continue on the faint path over the moor. Initially head towards Garsdale Station on the hillside ahead, then aim for the row of cottages at East Mud Becks as they come into view. A stile leads you out on to the A684. Turn right and then left up to the station.

Cautley Spout

Distance: 3¼ miles (5.25 km). Time: 2 hours.
Start/parking: free car park just past the Cross Keys Inn on the A683
Sedbergh–Kirkby Stephen road; grid ref 699969.
Terrain: footpaths, bridleways, short road and lane sections.
Height gained: 600 feet (180 m).
Public transport: bus 564 connects Penrith, Kendal and Kirkby Stephen
along the A683, and there is a bus stop at the start of the walk.
Facilities: the Cross Keys has all the usual facilities of an inn.
Map: OS Explorer OL19 – Howgill Fells & Upper Eden Valley.

This lovely walk sets off across a valley formed by glacial action (rare in these rounded hills), admires stunning waterfalls and mountain scenery close to, then crosses the valley to get a broader view of the full picture.

Descend steps leading down from the car park. Cross the footbridge over the River Rawthey. Follow the obvious path which has the river on the left. At a junction of paths, take the right-hand option heading away from the river. (You'll use the left-hand one in a while to continue the walk after walking up to the waterfalls.)

The path begins to ascend gently but is never too onerous. Two tiny becks are forded. Gradually more and more can be seen of Cautley Holme Beck as it cascades down the high, vertical camber in a series of stepped waterfalls, known as Cautley Spout. Although not shown on maps, a narrow path heads

The distinctive bubbling song of the curlew may be heard on the high moors during spring

21

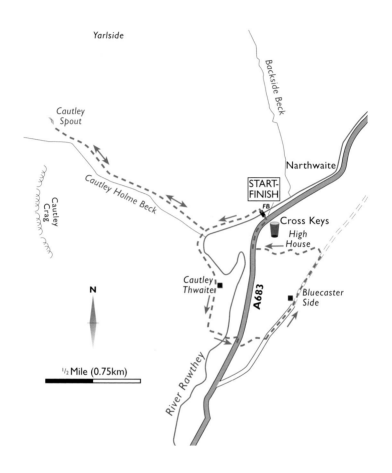

left towards and along the edge of the tree-lined gully. The smaller falls down below and Cautley Crag towering above can now be appreciated in their full glory.

Cautley Crag is a shoulder of the Calf, the highest of the Howgill Fells, and the exception to the Howgills' norm of smooth rounded heights. The Crag's rugged cliffs and corrie are the only notable evidence of glacial erosion in the whole group of hills, and create a breathtaking landscape viewed from this proximity.

Follow the narrow path as it veers right, back to the main path below where the land starts to rise steeply up the side of the higher waterfalls. Use the main path to return downhill. When you reach the junction of paths, now take the right-hand option.

Cross the footbridge over Cautley Holme Beck. Follow the footpath with a wall on the right and the River Rawthey on the left. Proceed through a gate. Where the path divides, take the left-hand option. Keep close to the River Rawthey and pass a barn on your right. The path is obvious as it leaves the

A walk to Cautley Spout is a highlight of any visit to the Howgill Fells.

river and heads south across fields. Pass the farm buildings at Cautley Thwaite. Cross a couple more fields. Swing left over the footbridge across the Rawthey. Exit on to the main A683 road just below High Wardses.

Turn right for a few paces. Cross over the road and go through a gate leading to a bridleway signposted 'Hollow Lane'; an appropriate name as the 'lane' is eroded and sunken, but can be avoided by using a higher-level path which works to the right and meets a metalled lane. Turn left.

This is the part of the walk that offers superb panoramic views across the valley to the waterfalls and fells beyond.

Follow the unfenced lane past Bluecaster Side, where it changes to a rough track heading on to open moorland. Continue until you reach a yellow marker-post. Turn sharply left as indicated. A grassy path descends past High House (which is just a barn) on your right and goes through a gate to the left. Continue downhill through another gate and out on to the A683 road. Turn right, back to the car park.

A circuit of Wandale Hill

Distance: 4½ miles (7 km). Time: 3–3½ hours.
Start/parking: free car park adjacent to the A683 Sedbergh–Kirkby Stephen
road 100 yards west of Rawthey Bridge; grid ref 711979.
Terrain: footpaths and tracks (some indistinct in parts), and short road
sections; this walk is quite challenging as it's in a remote area and crosses
open moorland, so would best be enjoyed during a spell of dry weather
and when there is clear visibility; good map-reading skills are essential.
Height gained: 950 feet (290 m).
Public transport: Bus 564 connects Brough, Sedbergh, Kendal and
Kirkby Stephen along the A683.
Facilities: none available.
Map: OS Explorer OL19 – Howgill Fells & Upper Eden Valley.

This walk, which takes in three farmsteads with 'thwaite' (meaning a clearing) in their name, takes you round the wilder side of Wandale Hill.

From the car park, turn left along the lane and cross Rawthey Bridge.

Rawthey Bridge is situated among delightful fells. The current bridge was built in 1822 and has a carved stone head below each parapet.

(Observe the footpath on the left immediately after the bridge, as this is the return route.) Continue along the lane for approximately ¼ mile (0.4 km) and take the next footpath on the left, signposted 'Murthwaite'. Cross the footbridge and head straight uphill. Go through a gate and on past a barn on the right. Cross a fence-stile, visible initially on the skyline. Bear right, then cross a wall-stile confirmed by a yellow marker arrow. Follow the path to the front of Murthwaite Farm. Proceed through a wide gate to the left of the buildings. Swing right, round the back, as directed by yellow marker-posts. Opposite the end of the buildings, swing left up a grassy track.

This track soon divides. Take the right option (which is virtually straight ahead), along a reedy, walled track. Cross a stile in the right-hand corner by a dilapidated barn. Keep ahead on an obvious tractor-track with a wall on the left most of the time. Bear left over the wall where indicated by a direction arrow. Traverse to the right across fields. This is one of the areas where the path is indistinct, but you can see the buildings at Adamthwaite in the distance ahead, which gives a good guide to where you should be heading.

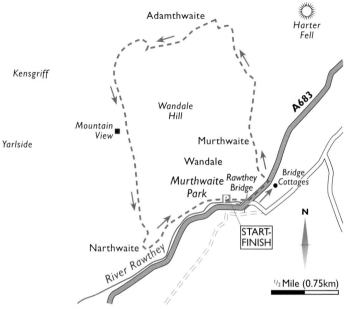

Adamthwaite still retains its spinning gallery on the front side of the house for, in the eighteenth and nineteenth centuries, agriculture only just exceeded the knitting of stockings and gloves as the main trade of the area.

Don't lose too much altitude as you traverse along the hillside, and don't be confused because the route on the ground varies from that on the OS map, as it has been re-routed to these higher contours. A faint trod does appear as you cross two broken walls. Head up round the top corner of the third wall. Descend over a poor stile. Cross another stile immediately to the right. Continue heading towards Adamthwaite by keeping close to the wall on the right. Take care as the land on the left drops steeply into the valley. Descend a little on a faint path which leads to a gate. A direction arrow points down to the left. A faint path does continue straight ahead, but ignore this and bear more to the left, following the direction indicated), keeping fairly close to a wall that doglegs. At the bottom, go through another gate and cross an old, narrow stone bridge. Head up towards the left-hand side of a barn. Enter the farmyard between the barn and a sheepfold. Turn right on the track passing the front of the farmhouse. Continue ahead to meet the end of the lane from Ravenstonedale.

For the inhabitants of Adamthwaite this 2½ mile (4 km) wafer of road is a vital link with the outside world for, even though the main A683 road passes within 1¼ miles (2 km) of the house, anyone approaching from the south has to take a long and circuitous route north and then west across to Raven-stonedale village, before heading south down this narrow lane.

Turn left up the stony track to a wide gate leading to moorland. Follow the track round to the right of a new barn to a large standing stone. Go through an old metal gate on the left, marked with a yellow arrow. Bear right along a tractor-track with a wall on the left. Descend through a gate. Ford a small beck, and keep ahead across the moor.

If the track becomes indistinct, bear slightly right towards the curved wall (marked 'Adamthwaite Sike' on the OS map) and you should pick the track up again coming in from the right. When you do, bear left and follow the track as it swings south and maintains altitude, with the land rising on the left, and falling to the valley on the right.

This is a grand section, with super views across the valley to Kensgriff and Yarlside, and gives an indication of the typical Howgill scenery of rounded fells above dark valleys.

The track becomes distinct with a wall on the right as the ruins of Mountain View are seen lower in the valley. Keep ahead where another path goes off left by an arrowed marker-post. Walk along a grassy path that gently descends. The roofs of Narthwaite Farm come into view. Enter the farmyard. Following the forward-facing yellow direction arrows on the left, go straight across to come out on to the farm drive. Walk downhill.

Leave the drive where it bears right, to go straight ahead across a field and through the right-hand one of a pair of gates. Ford Wandale Beck.

Don't despair if you've got as far as the ford at Wandale Beck and found it to be impassable. Retrace your steps to the farm track leading down from Narthwaite and turn left down to the road, where you turn left again back to the car park. (Please note that this alternative end to the route is with the kind permission of the farmers at Narthwaite, and kindly respect the fact that you are on private land.)

The path divides; take the right-hand option to enter a field and keep to the higher ground. Enter the delightful woodlands at the south of Murthwaite Park via a step-stile. Follow the obvious path along the bank of the River Rawthey (taking care as the land drops very steeply to the river at times). Cross a footbridge giving access back on to the A683. Turn right, over Rawthey Bridge, back to the car park.

Birkett Common

Distance: 4¼ miles (6.8 km). Time: 2–2½ hours.
Start/parking: on the B6259 Garsdale to Kirkby Stephen road at its
junction with Tommy Road opposite Pendragon Castle, where limited free
parking is available; grid ref 783027.
Terrain: footpaths, bridleways and quiet lanes; no stiles on this walk.
Height gained: 670 feet (205 m).
Public transport: none available.
Facilities: none available.
Map: OS Explorer OL19 – Howgill Fells & Upper Eden Valley.

*Located to the north of Mallerstang Dale's wild landscape, this circuit of
Birkett Common is packed with interest and history: a river, two ruined
castles, a lane built by soldiers — and giants' graves.*

Head up Tommy Road, passing Pendragon Castle on your left.

*With its stunning location and fabled connections with Uther Pendragon,
Pendragon Castle's enigmatic ruin oozes history and legend. Originally
built as a keep in the eleventh century, the castle was extended and restored
300 years later by Roger de Clifford after becoming the local seat of the
Clifford family (also owners of castles in Skipton, Appleby and Brougham).
But Pendragon fell into disuse again until its hard-fought-for inheritance by
Lady Anne Clifford, after which it became one of her favourite residences.*

The ruins of Pendragon Castle are a reminder of its former glories.

27

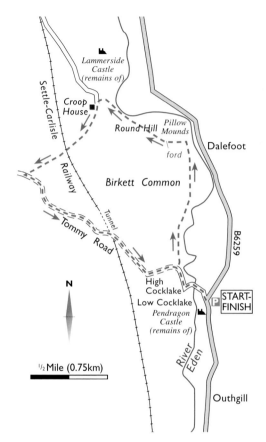

Lammerside
Castle
(remains of)

Settle-Carlisle

Croop
House

Round Hill

Pillow
Mounds

Dalefoot

ford

Railway

Birkett Common

Tommy Road

Tunnel

B6259

N

High
Cocklake

Low Cocklake

Pendragon
Castle
(remains of)

P START-
FINISH

½ Mile (0.75km)

River Eden

Outhgill

Sadly her progeny let it fall into ruin once more and Pendragon is in a dangerous condition now. Please note the castle is on private farmland.

Follow the lane as it crosses the River Eden. Leave the lane just after a cattle grid on a sharp left-hand bend, turning right along the bridleway signposted 'Wharton'. The wide, grassy track descends slightly and keeps the river down on the right for approximately ¾ mile (1.2 km) to Birkett Bottom (Dalefoot Farm is opposite). Bear left on a track beneath telegraph cables.

The Pillow Mounds shown on the map just north of here are Bronze Age burial mounds described as looking like large, shallow graves known locally as Giants' Graves.

Continue along the track. The River Eden comes close as the ruins of Lammerside Castle can be seen just ahead.

Although it's uncertain who built Lammerside Castle or why, legend refers to it being the seat of a Sir Tarquin who ate boys. Perhaps the story of it being the one-time home of the Wharton family is more feasible but, whatever its history, the castle has been in a ruinous state for approximately 500 years.

Continue over a flat concrete bridge and up a narrow field. Bear left opposite the castle (a yellow marker-post indicates the route). Walk up to the metalled lane in front of the partially whitewashed Croop House. Turn left along the lane, which soon becomes a rough track. Go through a narrow field with a wall on the right. Turn right, up a walled, grassy track by a large wooden barn. Proceed through two gates and on under the railway.

Meadow cranesbill has blueish-purple flowers.

This section of the Settle-Carlisle railway line runs between Dent and Kirkby Stephen and, so challenging were the conditions endured to lay the tracks, it took 6,000 navvies five years to complete the work.

The obvious path rises up through a reedy field, before joining a stronger track by a marker post. Here bear left, with a wall on the right, to Tommy Road. Turn left, noting the fine limekiln to the right.

Tommy Road, which links Ravenstonedale and Mallerstang Dale, was improved by soldiers (nicknamed Tommies – hence the name), who camped here during the First World War. From the high points are fine views to the north-west over Kirkby Stephen and the Pennines.

Follow the lane as it rises up, then levels, as the railway tunnel comes in on the right.

This is the 424-yard (388 m) long Birkett Tunnel, close to which were Birkett Huts — temporary accommodation for the navvies building the railway line and their families.

You get a good idea of the landscape of Mallerstang Dale as you descend down Tommy Road and past Pendragon Castle to the car park.

Ravenstonedale to Paradise

Distance: 3¾ miles (6 km). Time: 2 hours.
Start/parking: free car park adjacent to Ravenstonedale Primary School;
grid ref 723042.
Terrain: footpaths, bridleways and quiet lanes.
Height gained: 700 feet (215 m).
Public transport: Bus 564 connects Brough, Kendal, Sedbergh and
Kirkby Stephen with Ravenstonedale.
Facilities: pub and small shop in Ravenstonedale.
Map: OS Explorer OL19 – Howgill Fells & Upper Eden Valley.

Leave the car park in a south-easterly direction along the lane through Ravenstonedale, with Scandal Beck on the left. Pass the Black Swan and the junction with the Sedbergh road.

Rev William Nicholls wrote in 1850 in his History and Traditions of Ravenstonedale Volume II *that "The morals of the people are good and the farmers are thrifty and intelligent". At one time Ravenstonedale had three grocers, a butcher and slaughterhouse, a joiner, tailor, blacksmith, dress-maker, post office, various banks, a set of petrol pumps and a weekly market. Today it has just the Black Swan pub and adjacent small shop.*

Bear left along the road. Take the second footpath on the right (the one after you've crossed the bridge), signposted 'Low Lane'. A gate at the end of a wall to the right leads into a narrow field with the beck on your right, confirmed by a yellow marker-post. Go through another gate with a yellow marker. Turn right on to Low Lane opposite a barn.

After a few paces a footpath along a short, walled track on the right sign-posted 'Stouphill Gate and Bowber Head' should be your route, but it is impassable as a necessary bridge appears to have vanished. So the presumed route is to continue along the lane for a few paces, go through a gate on the right and cross the beck by a flat bridge. Turn left and aim for the corner of a cross-wall ahead down the field, keeping a narrow watercourse on your left.

Head to the right across the field to a fence and Scandal Beck on the right. Reach a gate in the right-hand corner. (Claylands Farm is across the lane on your left.) Continue ahead. The path crosses numerous fields, some reedy, some improved pastureland, with Scandal Beck always to the right. Stiles

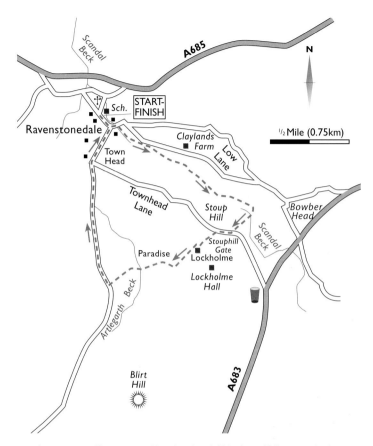

over the cross-walls are usually clearly visible but, if in any doubt, are always in the right-hand corner.

When you reach a field with a barn ahead, veer left to a stile in the left-hand wall where a row of trees ends. Cross the wooden footbridge ahead. Turn right. There is another small watercourse on your right, with the land on the left rising up. You'll soon reach a cross-wall where yellow marker arrows show that the path divides.

This border region of North Yorkshire and Cumbria is home to some of the last surviving colonies of red squirrel in England. Red squirrels, one of Britain's favourite native mammals, have had such a hard time over recent years due to loss of their woodland habitat and the introduction of grey squirrels (which compete for food and pass on a deadly disease called parapoxvirus), to the extent that greys now outnumber reds by sixty-six to one across the country.

Take the right-hand path. Soon cross a tiny watercourse via a stone bridge. Pass to the right of a barn. Cross two wooden bridges in quick succession. A step-stile leads into the corner of a field. Walk uphill to the top corner, with a fence and shrubs on the left. At a gate, keep uphill in the same direction. Head towards a stone barn, enjoying open views away to the left. Walk slightly right, away from the wall and barn, to a yellow marker. After a step-stile, bear slightly right to meet Townhead Lane via a narrow stile beside a gate.

Monkeyflower (front) and meadowsweet (back) are both found in damp areas.

Turn right on the lane. Go past Stouphill Gate Farm. Take a stony bridleway descending on the left, signposted 'Lockholme Hall'. Keep right where the track divides across a flat, concrete bridge. Dog-leg between the buildings at Lockholme. Swing left up to three gates. Take the middle one marked with a yellow arrow. Walk up the stony track between a wall and a fence to another marked gate. Keep straight ahead, and here it is: Paradise.

It may only be a small lake with waterfowl and views front-left to Harter Fell and across Mallerstang Dale to Wild Boar Fell, but it's rather heavenly and makes a good picnic spot.

Follow the track as it works right, round the lake. Rise up on a fainter tractor-track to a wall. Continue ahead, keeping the wall on your left. Beside a house, a yellow marker points straight ahead to a metal gate. This gives access to a track. Bear right, across Artlegarth Beck. Keep on to join a lane beside a chalet park. Turn right.

The stretch of the route along the lane is quiet and makes for good walking.

As you approach the village, bear right across a bridge back into Ravenstonedale. Pass a small green on the left. Keep on the lane through the village. Bear left past the Black Swan pub, and back to the car park.